THE
UNDRESSING

ALSO BY LI-YOUNG LEE

Behind My Eyes

Book of My Nights

The City in Which I Love You

Rose

The Winged Seed: A Remembrance

UNDRESSING

POEMS

LI-YOUNG LEE

W. W. NORTON & COMPANY

Independent Publishers Since 1923

New York | London

For information about permission to reproduce selections from this book,
write to Permissions, W. W. Norton & Company, Inc.,
500 Fifth Avenue, New York, NY 10110

For information about special discounts for bulk purchases, please contact
W. W. Norton Special Sales at specialsales@wwnorton.com or 800-233-4830

Manufacturing by Berryville Graphics
Book design by JAM Design
Production manager: Lauren Abbate

Library of Congress Cataloging-in-Publication Data

Names: Lee, Li-Young, 1957 – author
Title: The undressing : poems / Li-Young Lee
Description: First edition. | New York : W. W. Norton & Company, 2018
Identifiers: LCCN 2017051768 | ISBN 9780393065435 (hardcover)
Classification: LCC PS3562.E35438 A6 2018 | DDC 811/ .54—dc23
LC record available at https://lccn.loc.gov/2017051768

W. W. Norton & Company, Inc., 500 Fifth Avenue, New York, N.Y. 10110
www.wwnorton.com
W. W. Norton & Company Ltd., 15 Carlisle Street, London W1D 3BS

1 2 3 4 5 6 7 8 9 0

For The Lovers
And The Manifold Beloved

CONTENTS

I

THE UNDRESSING   *13*

II

SPOKEN FOR   *29*
I LOVED YOU BEFORE I WAS BORN   *31*
ADORE   *32*
CEREMONY OF THE INTENDED   *35*
STOLEN GOOD   *37*

III

OUR SECRET SHARE   *41*
FOLDING A FIVE-CORNERED STAR SO THE CORNERS MEET   *48*
GOD IS BURNING   *50*
THREE WORDS   *51*
LOVE SUCCEEDING   *54*
MY SWEET ACCOMPANIST   *56*
READING, COUNTING, PLAYING ALONE   *59*
HIS LIKENESS   *62*
HIDDEN HEARING   *64*
AT THE YEAR'S REVOLVING DOOR   *66*
LEAVING   *69*
EAVESDROPPING AT MORNING'S SILL   *70*
THE WORD FROM HIS SONG   *72*
ALL ABOUT THE BIRDS   *74*

IV

CHANGING PLACES IN THE FIRE   *79*
SANDALWOOD   *94*

ACKNOWLEDGMENTS   *95*

I

THE UNDRESSING

Listen,
she says.

I'm listening, I answer
and kiss her chin.

Obviously, you're not, she says.

I kiss her nose and both of her eyes.
I can do more than one thing at a time,
I tell her. Trust me.
I kiss her cheeks.

You've heard of planting lotuses in a fire, she says.
You've heard of sifting gold from sand.

You know
perfumed flesh, in anklets, and spirit, unadorned,
take turns at lead and follow,
one in action and repose.

I kiss her neck and behind her ear.

But there are things you need reminded of, she says.
So remind me, Love, I say.

There are stories we tell ourselves, she says.
There are stories we tell others.
Then there's the sum
of our hours
death will render legible.

I unfasten the top button of her blouse
and nibble her throat with more kisses.

Go on, I say, I'm listening.
You better be, she says,
you'll be tested.

I undo her second,
her third, fourth, and last buttons quickly,
and then lean in
to kiss her collarbone.

She says, The world
is a story that keeps beginning.
In it, you have lived severally disguised:
bright ash, dark ash, mirror, moon;
a child waking in the night to hear the thunder;
a traveler stopping to ask the way home.
And there's still
the butterfly's night sea-journey to consider.

She says,
There are dreams we dream alone.
There are dreams we dream with others.
Then there's the lilac's secret
life of fire, of God
accomplished in the realm
of change and desire.

Pushing my hand away from her breast,
she keeps talking.

Alone, you dream in several colors: Blue,
wishing, and following the river.

In company, you dream in several others:
The time you don't have.
The time left over.
And the time it takes.

Your lamp has a triple wick:
Remembering, questioning, and sheltering
made of your heart's and mind's agreement.
With it, you navigate the two seas: Day
with everything inside it;
night and all that's missing.

Meanwhile, I encounter difficulty
with her skirt knot, her fingers
confounding my progress,
as she goes on reviewing the doubtful points.

There are words we say in the dark.
There are words we speak in the light.
And sometimes they're the same words.

From where I've been sitting beside her,
I drop to one knee before her.

There's the word we give
to another.
There's the word we keep
with ourselves.
And sometimes they're the same word.

I slip one hand inside her blouse
and find her naked waist.
My other hand cradles her bare foot
from which her sandal has fallen.

A word has many lives.
Quarry, the word is game, unpronounceable.
Pursuant, the word is judge, pronouncing sentence.
Affliction, the word is a thorn, chastising.

I nudge her blouse open with my nose
and kiss her breastbone.

The initiating word
embarks, fixed between sighted wings, and
said, says, saying, none are the bird,
each just moments of the flying.

Doubling back, the word is infinite.
We circle ourselves,
the fruit rots in time,
and we're just passengers of our voices,
a bird in one ear crying, *Two!*
There are two worlds!
A bird in the other ear urging, *Through!*
Be through with this world and that world!

Her blouse lapses around her shoulders,
and I bend lower
to kiss her navel.

There are voices that wake us in the morning, she says.
There are voices that keep us up all night.

I lift my face and look into her eyes. I tell her,
The voices I follow
to my heart's shut house say,
A member of the late
and wounded light enjoined to praise,
each attends a song that keeps leaving.

Now, I'm fondling her breasts
and kissing them. Now,
I'm biting her nipples.
Not meaning to hurt her,
I'm hurting her a little,
and for these infractions I receive
the gentlest tugs at my ear.

She says,
All night, the lovers ask, *Do you love me?*
Over and over, the manifold beloved answers,
I love you. Back and forth,
merging, parting, folding, spending,
the lovers' voices
and the voices of the beloved
are the ocean's legion scaling earth's black bell,
their bright crested foam
the rudimentary beginnings
of bridges and wings, the dream of flying,
and the yearning to cross over.

Now, I'm licking her armpit. I'm inhaling
its bitter herbal fumes and savoring
its flavor of woodsmoke. I've undone
the knot to her skirt.

Bodies have circled bodies
from the beginning, she says,

but the voices of lovers
are Creation's most recent flowers, mere buds
of fire nodding on their stalks.

In love, we see
God burns hidden, turning
inside everything that turns.

And everything turns. Everything
is burning.

But all burning is not the same.
Some fires kindle freedom.
Some fires consolidate your bondage.
Do you know the difference?

I tell her, I want you to cup your breasts
in both of your hands
and offer them to me.
I want you to make them wholly
available to me.

I want to be granted open liberty
to leave many tiny
petal-shaped bruises,
like little kisses, all over you.

One and one is one, she says.
Bare shineth in bare.

Think, she says, of the seabirds
we watched at dawn
wheeling between that double blue
above and below them.

Defined by the gravity they defy,
they're the radiant shadows of what they resist,

and their turns and arcs in air
that will never remember them
are smiles on the face of the upper abyss.

Their flying makes
our inner spaciousness visible,
even habitable, restoring us
to infinity, we beings of nonbeing,
each so recent a creature,
and only lately spirits
learning how to love.

Shrill, their winged hungers
fill the attic blue
and signal our nagging jeopardy:
Death's bias, the slope
of our lives' every minute.

I want to hear you utter
the sharpest little cries of tortured bliss, I say,
like a slapped whelp spurt
exquisite gasps of delighted pleasure.

But true lovers know, she says,
hunger vacant of love is a confusion,
spoiling and squandering
such fruit love's presence wins.

The harvest proves the vine
and the hearts of the ones who tend it.

Everything else is gossip, guessing
at love's taste.

The menace of the abyss will be subdued, I say,
when I extort from you the most lovely cries
and quivering whispered pleas
and confused appeals of, *Stop*, and, *More*, and, *Harder.*

To love, she says. For nothing.
What birds, at home in their sky,
have dared more?

What circus performer,
the tent above him, the net below,
has risked so much? What thinker, what singer,
both trading for immortality?

Nothing saves him who's never loved.
No world is safe in that one's keeping.

We are travelers among other travelers
in an outpost by the sea.
We meet in transit, strange to each other,
like birds of passage between a country and a country,
and suffering from the same affliction of sleeplessness,
we find each other in the night
while others sleep. And between
the languages you speak and the several I remember,
we convene at the one we have in common,
a language neither of us was born to.
And we talk. We talk with our voices,
and we talk with our bodies.
And behind what we say,
the ocean's dark shoulders rise and fall all night,
the planet's massive wings ebbing and surging.

I tell her, Our voices shelter each other,
figures in a dream of refuge
and sanctuary.

Therefore, she says,
designations of North, South, East, and West,
Winter, Spring, Summer, Fall,

first son, second son, first daughter, second daughter,
change, but should correspond
to a current picture of the sky.

Each of our days fulfills
the measures of the sanctum
and its great tables' rounds.
The tables are not round.
Or, not only round.
At every corner,
opposites emerge, and you meet yourself.

I bow my head
and raise her foot to my mouth.

The pillared tables make a tower and a ladder.
They constitute the altar, the throne, and the crown.
The crown is not for your
head. The throne is not your seat.
The days on which the altar stands
will be weighed and named.
And the days are not days.
Not the way you might understand days.
The altar summons the feast
and is an aspect of the host.

The smell of her foot
makes me think of saddles.
I lick her instep. I kiss her toes. I kiss her ankle.

Don't you kiss my lips
with that mouth, she says.

Gold bit, I think.
Tender spur, I think.

I kiss her calves. I kiss her knees.
I kiss the insides of her thighs.
I'm thinking about her hip bones. I'm tonguing
the crease where her thigh and her belly meet.

The rounds enclose the dance,
she says.

The round and the square together
determine the dimensions of the ark, she says.
The water is rising as we speak.

Are you paying attention? she says,
One and one is two.
You and me are three. A long arithmetic
no temporal hand reckons
rules galaxies and ants, exact
and exacting. Lovers obey,
sometimes contradicting human account.

The smell of her body
mixes with her perfume and makes me woozy.

All being tends toward fire, I say.

All being tends toward fire,
sayeth the fire, she says, correcting me.

All being tends toward water, sayeth the water,
Light, sayeth the light.
Wings, sayeth the birds.
Voice, sayeth the voiceless.

Give up guessing, she says, give up
these frightened gestures of a stooped heart.
You've done all your learning with others in mind.

You've done all your teaching thinking only of yourself.
Saving the world, you oppress people.
Abandon educated words and honored acts.
I want you to touch me
as if you want to know me, not arouse me.
And by God, sing! For nothing. Singing
is origin. Out of that modulated trembling, cosmic
and rooted in the primordial, quantum and concealed
in the temporal, all forms come to be.
Each thing, born of the myriad in concert, is one song
variously sung. Each thing flourishes by singing
and returns to vanish into song.

Your body is that whereby song is conducted.
Singing is that whereby your body is completed.
Singing develops all things.
Dying is singing's consummation.
Thinking, you remain entangled
in the coils of your world.
Singing, you marry all possible worlds.

You know, from all of your green and branching hours
that so soon die unremarked, general and redundant,
the hours you sing return to you in true scale and degree.
The hours you measure by singing return winged
and noted, throated, eyed, and whirring-hearted.
Return red-crested, blue-feathered, black-frocked,
striped, spotted, flecked, and fine-boned.
But don't stop there. Sing the tree,
sing the All, sing the lot
of your time, and uncover the body of the Word,
the compass of compasses. Sing change
and the principle of wings, the laws of seeing and hearing,
rising and falling, harmony and strife. Sing all
the ungraspable, the descending, ascending signatures,
and you sing the name of life.

Call everyone of you to the feast.

Now, I'm drooling along her ribs.
I'm smacking my lips and tongue to better taste
her mossy, nutty, buttery, acrid sweat.

I know you more than I know, she says.
My body, astonished, answers to your body
without me telling it to.

Inside her is the safest place to be.
Inside her, with all those other mysteries,
those looming immensities:
god, time, death, childhood.

Listen, she says,
There's one more thing.
Regarding the fires, there are two.
Left and right, they grow wiser in the same house.
Up and down, the higher encases the lower,
and the lower clings to the higher.
Inner and outer, these two illuminations
are a thousand illuminations.

But I'm thinking,
My hands know things my eyes can't see.
My eyes see things my hands can't hold.

Listen, she says,
Never let the fires go out.
The paler, the hotter.

But I'm thinking, Pale alcove.
I'm thinking, My heart ripens with news
the rest of me waits to hear.

Are you listening?
But I'm not listening.
I'm thinking,

A nest of eggs for my crown, please.
And for my cushion, my weight in grapes.

I'm thinking, In one light,
love might look like siege.
In another light, rescue
might look like danger.

She says, The seeds of fire are ours to mother.

The dust, the shavings,
and all spare materials
must be burned in both fires,
the visible and the invisible.

Even the nails burned in them.
Even the tools burned.
And then the oven dismantled and burned.
Have you been hearing me?

For 20,000 years, human groups have thrived
by subtle and not so subtle mechanisms
of expulsion, exclusion, rejection, elimination, and murder.
Fractious multitudes made single
by false transcendences of state
and race. Unruly, disputatious, opining smithereens
and fractions come together over a sacrificial corpse,
a field of corpses, the earth covered with sacrifices.
Rivalrous fragments banded by irresistible want.
Legion united by unbounded appetite and fear
spawning new gods and false prophets every day.

Repugnant little pleasure machines,
mesmerized minions of the marketplace, sold
desire, sold conflict by greedy advertisers,
leaving love waxed cold in your wake,
famine, pestilence, and earthquakes your wake,
abomination, desolation, and tribulation your wake.
Violence your wake. One nation under the weapon.
One human city under the banner of murder.
One kalpa under the stumbling block.
One world under the sign of the scapegoat.
One species under the flag of the goat's head.
Well, it's too late for flags.
It's too late
for presidents. It's too late
for movie stars and the profit economy.
It's too late for plutonomy and precariate.
The war is on.
If love doesn't prevail,
who wants to live in this world?
Are you listening?

You thought my body was a tree
in which lived a bird. But now, can't you see
flocks alive in this blazing foliage?
Blue throngs, gold multitudes, and pale congregations.
And each member flits from branch to living branch.
Each is singing at different amplitudes and frequencies.
Each is speaking secrets that will ripen into sentence.
And their voices fan my fragrant smoldering.
Disclosing the indestructible body of law.
Ratifying ancient covenants. Establishing new cities.
And their notes time the budding
of your own flowering.
Die now. And climb up into this burning.

II

SPOKEN FOR

I didn't know I was blue,
until I heard her sing.

I was never aware so much
had been lost
even before I was born.
There was so much to lose
even before I knew
what it meant to choose.

Born blue,
living blue unconfessed, blue
in concealment, I've lived all my life
at the plinth
of greater things than me.

Morning is greater
with its firstborn light and birdsong.
Noon is taller, though a moment's realm.
Evening is ancient and immense, and
night's storied house more huge.

But I had no idea.
And would have died without a clue,
except she began to sing. And I understood

my soul is a bride enthralled by an unmet groom,
or else the groom wholly spoken for, blue
in ardor, happy in eternal waiting.

I heard her sing and knew
I would never hear the true

name of each thing
until I realized the abysmal
ground of all things. Her singing
touched that ground in me.

Now, dying of my life, everything is made new.
Now, my life is not my life. I have no life
apart from all of life.

And my death is not my death,
but a pillow beneath my head, a rock
propping the window open
to admit the jasmine.

I heard her sing,
and I'm no longer afraid.
Now that I know what she knows, I hope
never to forget
how giant the gone
and immaculate the going.
How much I've already lost.
How much I go on losing.
How much I've lived
all one blue. O, how much
I go on living.

eath, eyes, evanescent,
th, nowhere stored,
hers within its fondling

and gathering
 of Love's gaze, and only this,
1's audience, is the founding
he fundamental
id I say paradise?
ox . . . the fundamental paradox
 we breathe,
ve witness,
exchange,
m you write.

I LOVED YOU BEFORE I WAS BORN

I loved you before I was born.
It doesn't make sense, I know.

I saw your eyes before I had eyes to see.
And I've lived longing
for your every look ever since.
That longing entered time as this body.
And the longing grew as this body waxed.
And the longing grows as this body wanes.
That longing will outlive this body.

I loved you before I was born.
It makes no sense, I know.

Long before eternity, I caught a glimpse
of your neck and shoulders, your ankles and toes.
And I've been lonely for you from that instant.
That loneliness appeared on earth as this body.
And my share of time has been nothing
but your name outrunning my ever saying it clearly.
Your face fleeing my ever
kissing it firmly once on the mouth.

In longing, I am most myself, rapt,
my lamp mortal, my light
hidden and singing.

I give you my blank heart.
Please write on it
what you wish.

ADORE

(adore, verb, from Latin, *adorare*,
from *ad*- 'to' + *orare*- 'speak, call, pray')

You lie asleep beside me,
one hand on the pillow and cupped
at your mouth, as if to tell a secret.

As if you might say in your sleep
what you could never find
words for awake.

Or as if you called
across a din of other voices,
or the howl of empty space. Calling

because there are no bells
to strike the hours where we live. And I must know
when to kneel and when to rise.
What to praise and what to curse.
I must know how to bless
and how to receive blessing.

One hand on your pillow and cupped
at your mouth,
as if you spoke a word
you'd kept to yourself all day, waiting
for your most unguarded moment
to say, a thought meant for me, meant to be
shared between us this way,
sealed this way, a secret

no voice can carry without
a word without carriage, e
in the peace of your body

a word born out of your de
which only my own deepes
and happiest rest beside yo
face to face, free of thinkin

Maybe you had to be aslee
to say what you knew to be
Or what you had to say
you might not could bear t
and so must say so softly
I must close my eyes, I mu
inward, to where you've ma
and a bed inside me, to rec

You say:
We cannot look upon Love'
So we face each other to se
And thus third-person souls
suddenly stand at gaze
and the lover and the belov
second- and first-persons,
You and I, eye
to eye, are born.
But such refraction, multip
Love's eye upon the objects
as upon the objects of our r

My brush, hairpin, mirror, b
your loving look finds each
lovable, I can see. Things
by any other measure poor,
to make them your heart's

Face, blush
pledged to
Love's look
to adore.

This strewi
of Love's fa
begun in d
action, call
paradise . .
I meant pa
of the brea
the though
the kisses
and every

CEREMONY OF THE INTENDED

The morning I died was the day we wed, Love.

Falling from my father's apple tree,
it wasn't the bright gazes
of the pink and white blossoms
killed me. Nor was it
by the glare of their unblinking stares I perished.
It wasn't their lightning felled me,
rung my head like a bell.
And it was not the earth.
Never blame the earth.
What seizes the eye is never guilty
as the eye is guilty.

Coming back to life
in my mother's lap, I heard astonished voices swarm
like bees throughout the sunlit branches,
whispering, "He's awake."
"He'd turned blue, he'd stopped breathing."
"Now, he'll remember he's betrothed."
"Now, he'll know the names of things."
"Now, he'll write and read."
That was the morning of the day
you and I first married.

Do you remember my proposal
on the hill behind my parents' house?
Do you remember the paper ring
I offered you, setting it on a scale?
And your glad acceptance,
raising your childish heart, so light,
onto the opposite pan?

And your heart's sudden gravity sunk that pan.
And the ring turned gold.

Love, I remember,
after our secret ceremony on that windy hilltop,
I heard my name, and I turned and ran
toward the ones who called me back,

toward lights lit and voices congregating
at a long table spread for a meal under a tree.
I flew down, knowing
we were promised to each other before time.

STOLEN GOOD

I flushed twin doves
from my father's unmown field.
I missed them with my rocks and sling,
but brought them to their knees
with a shout of my father's name.

This was before rivers had names
other than names for my father.
It was even before there were numbers,
those fearsome first angels.
Well before the wind learned to speak
in the past tense,
long before it started crossing
into the future
by leaving behind all of its faces but one.

Watching my quarry tumble down the sky,
I began to long
to be born, to become
one of the heirs to the sorrows
of hunger, the rites of slaughter,
and the several names of desire and death.

The nearer I came to the place
where my game lay stunned, the more I yearned
for a new reckoning of fire and clay,
a new ratio of body and song,
just proportions of world and cry.

By the time I knelt over my spoil,
all of the light had withdrawn

to above the trees
and become an immense, bright ghost in the sky.

In the rearing shadow of the earth,
I stood up, my voice fugitive, my name vagabond,
a cursed and grieving brother
of every winged thing.

Inheritor of the sign of the violent
and the victim,
I awaited my true bride.

III

OUR SECRET SHARE

1.

Was it Vladimir Lenin said,
You have to crack a few
eggs to make an omelet?

It was Thomas Jefferson counseled, The tree of liberty
must be periodically watered with blood.

And to begin the first Crusade
in the eleventh century, Pope Urban II declared,
God wills it!

And to begin the Albigensian Crusade
in the thirteenth century, papal legate Arnaud Amalric,
in a white choir robe, urged the doubtful soldiers,
Kill them all!
Let God sort out His own!

War can only be abolished through war,
and in order to get rid of the gun, you must
take up the gun, said Chairman Mao.

And Friedrich Nietzsche wrote,
Weak and base, pity stands opposed
to the restorative emotions which heighten vitality.
We are deprived of life when we feel pity.

Funny, the things you remember,
lying awake at night.

2.

The Solo is a river in Indonesia.
My sister crosses it on a narrow skiff
piloted by a ferryman in a grass hat.
Behind him, she stands
still and straight beside her bicycle.
Their reflections slide along beneath them in the water.
And I wait for her.

My sister is in possession of one part
of a word
whose other part is in my keeping.
And as long as she never arrives,
as long as she never reaches the bank
on which I stand in recess from the minutes,
the ferryman will never lift her bicycle
out of the boat to set it on the ground,
my sister will never lay a coin in the man's open palm,
then jump onto the bike with me on the back,
and we'll never ride together home
to find the revolution has just begun,
liberation is at hand,
and the killing has already started
and will go on into the night
and the next day, night and day, day and night.
Funny, as long as her portion of the word
and my portion of the word
remain separate shares,
day never turns into night,
and my sister remains balanced forever
in the air above the watery girl
upside down below her,
and nobody dies.

3.

My childhood is two facing pages
in The Book of Childhood.

Open, the left-hand page begins:
They hated us without a cause.

And the right-hand page ends:
The fire had not harmed our bodies,
nor was a hair of our heads singed.

Funny, each one born receives
two pages in that great book,
and neither page is written by the child.

4.

After nineteen months in prison, eight of those in a leper
colony—and he never got leprosy—my father was
unrecognizable to me. So when I spied my mother slipping
him a bar of soap during our visit, at which time we were
allowed to stroll the prison yard together, I thought that
strange man had thieved it from her. As the guards were
returning him to his cell, I ran after them and snatched the
soap out of my father's pocket, exposing my parents' ploy. The
guards had a good laugh when they discovered what was
happening. Funny thing is, my father later told me, they didn't
punish him that time, though in the past he'd been tortured
for lesser offenses. The reason was he'd been teaching the
prison guards in secret, at their request, to read and write in
English, using the King James Bible.

5.

And my brother says, When I heard the student mob stampeding up
the apartment building's stairwell that morning, I jumped out of
bed, pulled on my shoes, and crawled out of my bedroom window.
Crouched on a ledge, undetected, I saw, through a neighbors'
kitchen window, catty-cornered one floor below, their grandmother
in a chair surrounded by angry students carrying wooden clubs,
metal pipes, and kitchen knives. Dressed in school uniforms,
middle- and high-school-aged, they were all shouting at the old
woman when one of them hit her across both eyes with his club, not
so hard as to knock her out, but hard enough her nose began to
bleed, and she cried out, "I can't see! I can't see!" at which those
children burst out laughing. Startled, I fell backwards off the ledge
into some trees growing along the hill behind the building. Funny
thing is, falling through the treetops saved my life, but plunging
through the branches pulled my pajama pants nearly off, and when
the old lady started really screaming—I guess by then they must
have begun stabbing her, I mean, I heard later that when her son
found her, she was full of holes, her body sticky with blood and
gaping wounds—anyway, I could hear her howling and begging even
as I tumbled down the hill head over heels, one shoe on, one shoe
flying in the air, my pants around my knees, and my dick out and
slapping every which way. I must have rolled for a hundred yards
like that before I hit the bottom. When I got back to my feet, I pulled
up my pants and raised my eyes to see a crowd of young
revolutionaries standing along the ridge of the slope, all of them
armed, all of them pointing at me and hurling insults. The hillside
was too long and steep for them to follow me, and I bolted with my
one shoe. I kept running for three days.

After he stops laughing, my brother asks, Hey, did I ever tell you
about the time I fainted while hiding in an outhouse and woke
up covered in piss? I'd passed out from the smell and weeks of
hunger on the road.

6.

Funny. Add them up, and the sleepless nights
of each brief life
amount to less than brief.
And yet, the while of each watch can so outstretch
all reach of counting, measure, or bearing
we find ourselves beyond
compass or echo

location, too late for childhood,
too early for God,
and Man only a possibility.

7.

Funny. Each night that I fall asleep to the sound of rain,
I think I'll wake up the following morning in a meadow,

part of an old stone wall,
robed in clover,
a willow king at the scarecrow ball.

8.

My brother telephones from China and it's dawn there.
The tea growers are picking the leaves
along tiered slopes of green hills
south of the city where he
and our mother were born.

Where I am, apple blossoms are flying
in the moonlight. The falling petals make a river glimpsed

through trees. They are a girl going
a little at a time. They signal
a later ripening, consummation, and greater commencement.

My brother says, "I'll drink three cups
alone this morning,
one for you, one for her, and one for me."

He tells me if I go to the window and look
I'll see the gibbous moon's gray face
and part of the darker
face behind it I almost know.
"Look at the moon," he says, "Mark the time."

Funny. Between my brother and I,
the one who's dreaming is still alive,
while the one who's dead is just beginning his day.

Between two brothers, both beyond time,
the dead one is afraid the living one will be late.
While the one who's alive goes on talking in his sleep.

I think I'll go to the window
and beg the moon for three apples from her trove.
One for the living, one for the dead, and one for you.

9.

My mother hangs her small hand
on the back of my neck and leans
forward to rest her forehead to my forehead.
I hold her other hand in both of mine.
Thus we sit, breathe together,
and neither of us speaks.

Funny. There are tears a mother must singly weep.
There are tears a son must weep by himself.
There are tears a woman must unaccompanied weep.
There are tears only a man in secret can weep.

My mother lives in possession
of one part of something unspeakable,
the other part of which
I keep, her gift to me. And as long
as what she won't say
and what I'll never tell
remain our secret share
of the world's unread history,
the unspoken weds the unspoken
face to face in the silence between us,
and both of our hearts knit
to remain intact.

Both of us will have to wait
until we're each alone to weep.

FOLDING A FIVE-CORNERED STAR SO THE CORNERS MEET

This sadness I feel tonight is not my sadness.

Maybe it's my father's.
For having never been prized by his father.
For having never profited by his son.

This loneliness is Nobody's. Nobody's lonely
because Nobody was never born
and will never die.

This gloom is Somebody Else's.
Somebody Else is gloomy
because he's always someone else.

For so many years, I answered to a name,
and I can't say who answered.

Mister Know Nothing? Brother Inconsolable?
Sister Every Secret? Anybody? Somebody?

Somebody thinks:
With death for a bedfellow,
how could thinking be anything but restless?

Somebody thinks: *God, I turn my hand facedown*
and You are You and I am me.

I turn my hand faceup
and You are the I
and I am your Thee.

What happens when you turn your hand?

Lord, remember me.
I was born in the City of Victory,
on a street called Jalan Industri, where
each morning, the man selling rice cakes went by
pushing his cart, its little steamer whistling,
while at his waist, at the end of a red string,
a little brass bell
shivered into a fine, steady seizure.

This sleeplessness is not my sleeplessness.
It must be the stars' insomnia.
And I am their earthbound descendant.

Someone, Anyone, No One, me, and Someone Else.
Five in a bed, and none of us can sleep.
Five in one body, begotten, not made.
And the sorrow we bear together is none of ours.
Maybe it's Yours, God.
For living so near to Your creatures.
For suffering so many incarnations unknown to Yourself.
For remaining strange to lovers and friends,
and then outliving them and all of their names for You.
For living sometimes for years without a name.
And all of Your springtimes disheveled.
And all of Your winters one winter.

GOD IS BURNING

Through an open wound in God's left side,
springtime enters into the world,
sticky, green, with a taste of iron.
That's not the wound I hurt from.

There's a dull pain in God's right hip,
around which throbbing axis
all worlds, visible and invisible, revolve.
That's not the pain that keeps me awake at night.

God is poor, naked, and alone.
But not the way the wren is poor.
And even the wood thrush has feathers.
Even mice have coats. Even cows have hides.

And God's not alone the way I'm alone,
my whole life merely a commentary on those verses:
You are as close to us as breathing, yet
You are farther than the farthermost star.

The sigh God sighed long ago
birthed lighted eons dying in time.
The sigh I sigh upon remembering Cain was my brother,
and so was Abel, fans every lit cell of me,

breathing, naked, hungry, thirsty, and sore
since birth, into an open tear, a burning tear
through which God surveys creation,
each a wet and living eye
in which God binds the Alpha and the Omega.

THREE WORDS

God-My-Father gave me three words:
O-My-Love.
O-My-God.
Holy-Holy-Holy.

God-My-Mother's wounds will never heal.

God-My-Brother is always alone in the library.

Meanwhile, I can't remember
how many brothers I have.

God-My-Sister, combing the knots out of my hair,
says that's because
so many brothers died before I learned to count,
and the ones who died after I acquired arithmetic
so exceeded the number of brothers still alive.

God-My-Father gave me three words to live by.
O-My-Love. O-My-God. Holy-Holy-Holy.

Why won't God-My-Mother's wounds heal?
Wounding myself doesn't cauterize her wounds.
Another wound to her won't seal her open blooms.

Her voice is a flowering tree struck by lightning.
It goes on greening and flowering,
but come petal-fall, its blossoms dropping
thunder so loud I must cover my ears to hear her.

Meanwhile, God-My-Brother spends every afternoon
alone with the books God-My-Father writes.

Some days he looks up
from a page, wearing the very face of horror.
Ask him what's the matter
and he'll stare into your eyes and whisper, "Murder!"
He'll howl, "Murder!" He'll scream, "Murder!"
Until he's hoarse or exhausted.
Or until God-My-Sister sits him down,
combs and braids his hair,
and sorts his dreams.

I'm counting out loud all of my brothers' names,
the living and the dead, on my fingers.
But the list is long,
leading back to the beginning
of the building of the first human cities,
and I keep losing my place and starting over.
Once, I remembered them all
except the first pair.

God-My-Sister says I must never say those names, never
pronounce the names of that first pair of brothers
within earshot of God-My-Brother.

God-My-Father gave me only three words.
How will I ever learn to talk like other people?

God-My-Mother sings, and her voice
comes like winter to break open the seeds.

God-My-Brother spends most of his time alone.
God-My-Sister is the only one
he'll ever let touch his face.

God-My-Sister, you should see her.
I have so many brothers,

but forever there will be
only one of her, God-My-Sister.

God-My-Father says from those three words
he gave me, all other words descend, branching.
That still leaves me unfit
for conversation, like some deranged bird
you can't tell is crying in grief or exultation,
all day long repeating,
"O my God. O my love. Holy, holy, holy."

LOVE SUCCEEDING

I don't know what makes God happy.
But my father in profile,
asleep on his back in the afternoon,
is a house with a river behind it.

The name of the river changes
by what it says
and the language you know.
The path to the orchard is overgrown.

And the child asleep beside him, its head
on his right shoulder, is gold
the bees harvest
to tip the scales weighing laughter and worry.

I don't know who God thinks is worth saving.
But my father drowsing
at a train window
impersonates the rain.

At rest, confirmed in a name, *Father*,
his true state remains unknown.
In transit, undocumented, unverified, illegal,
scapegoat, torture victim, fugitive, and refugee,
he sleeps, escaped,
momentarily unclaimed and out of favor.

Only he and God know
he's changed his name again to flee
yet another country.

And the boy awake
and singing beside him is several things:
An expert at tying and untying knots.
A traveler stranded on that ancient peak
called Father's Heart.
A hidden fruit distilling light and time
to render news of the living.

And my memories are precious
to no one but myself.
My feelings are holy
to no one but myself.

And I don't know
what might bring peace on earth. But a man
fallen asleep at his desk while revising
a letter to his father is apple blossoms
left lying where they fell.

The son who comes to wake him by kissing
the crown of his head is so many things:
Love succeeding.
The eye of the needle.
Little voice calling the flowers to assembly.

May the child never forget the power of the small.
May the man never wake a stranger to himself.

MY SWEET ACCOMPANIST

We were alive together once.
I thought it was that way from the beginning
of time. And I sang
my songs for him, and he rocked,
squeezing and pulling the accordion in his lap,
while his eyes glistened, shining.

My singing done, he stopped and looked away,
wiped his eyes, then turned
another face to me.
And he said,

"I don't need to hear your descriptions of my garden.
I planted everything in that garden.
I can read each leaf and bud
by sunlight, by moonlight, and by no light.
You think I don't know what's in my garden?
Or who or what's been there?
I taught you to love your neighbor.
Write a song about that."

Two fathers in one, I was their son,
we three alive together
in one space two at a time,
each of us taking his turn
alone in a double shadow.
He and I, and him remaindered.
Both of him, and me carried, carrying.
From the beginning of time.

And I thought it would be forever
I would sing for them,

my father in tears, whose fingers jumped
up and down the black and white keys,
and my father who waited
for the end of my song to say:

"I don't need to hear about your categories:
Sacred/profane.
Concrete/abstract.
Self/not self.
Nature/not nature.
Past/present/future.

Where your cleverness can't reach,
there are victims in the world without a defender.
The accusers are full of passion.
The persecutors hated us without a cause.
The ones who know not what they do are fierce,
though sometimes they apologized before murdering their prey.

Yet, I taught you to renounce violence.
I taught you love means to vest your interest
in the outcome of the other.
Desire means deriving
pleasure from the other.
I taught you to distinguish
poison from elixir, salt from decay.
Degree, degree, degree.
Write a song about that."

A boy becomes a young man in an instant.
But not before he learns to say yes to life
is to say yes to death.
To say no to death
is to say no to living.

A young man becomes an old man even quicker.
But not before he gives up life
and death, yes and no.

These days, it's one in the light, and two in the dark.
Or two beyond light and dark,
and one still subject wondering
in what key my one of two fathers would play,
and what would the other of that stubborn pair say
if they could hear the song I wrote just yesterday,

a song in which the people
are the same size as the animals and the trees,
and all of them are the same size as the sun.
And every living thing is crying with its mouth wide open.
Blue tears the size of giant petals are spurting
from the eyes of the sun,
from the eyes of the trees,
from the eyes of the grass,
and from the eyes of the four-legged
standing on four feet,
and from the eyes of the four-legged
standing on two feet,
and from the eyes of the two-legged
standing with hands and arms raised.

One remains and carries the two,
so I won't say I'm fatherless,
though I've been singing to myself for years now
without my father's playing, that sweet accompanist
and sad witness, wounded plaintiff, now silent
casualty of the twentieth century.

READING, COUNTING, PLAYING ALONE

Tossing the ball with both hands,
skyward higher and higher, the child
confides it to falling, not flying, gravity
the mother of this, his favorite toy.
Any wings inside him and unfledged, any flight
his own breathing's tendency
to measure distances by degrees of blue
and the irretrievable.

In the schoolroom, seated beside the open windows,
he's easily distracted by birds
in each day's margins. There,
his listening thrives.
The strife and hunger of those fierce cries
repeat his own heart's clamor, desire
and disappointment becoming
the ghost-score of every song
he'll learn to sing by eye or ear,
every note he'll count
during time's reign. And his life
grows shorter
each day he grows taller.
And whatever God or disembodied companion he speaks to
is left outside the schoolroom door each morning,
to be met again later on the walk home by himself
along the railroad tracks,
or in the sunlit aisles of the one-room public library,
or among the deer feeding in the cemetery.

Behind each child alone
at play or reading quietly,

stand the adults praying, or wringing their hands,
or pronouncing blessings, or making bets.
How long before he gives up believing
the dead are those who've flown
from our tended parks and gardens
to sing in the woods?
How soon before he'll quit
thinking the dead withdraw into the future
to prepare a place for the quick,
the wake of their going the train
he hears each evening, traveling
opposite the call to supper?

But this child knows to be silent, knows
not all elders are wise.
He knows better than to speak
of any wish in his custody, any hope
his secret brooding upon
might bring to term as trust.

Yet, it isn't true the dead have nothing to teach him.
He still doesn't know what to do
with his hands, those solemn ornaments,
in their presence.

You'd think many deaths early in life,
you'd think having to be silent and still in his father's arms when
carried away for good
from his native city littered with corpses,
would have taught this young one how to count
the uncountable,
how to hold the immeasurably heavy
in two hands when observing
falling bodies lit to rest in ceremonial rooms.
But watch him with his ball.
He's still learning.

He doesn't number his throws, rather
only what falls into his hands.

At play, before discriminations of *inside* and *outside*;
while reading, beyond estrangements of *life* from *after life*,
a whole world is his
to nurse at in sincere forgetfulness,
life and death seamless, one water lapsing
beneath no sky and four seasons.

But in his game, falling is return,
a second movement completing that first arising
in which the plunging back is pre-figured,
and the ball's leave-taking ascent from his hands
is powered by his own muster.
He's only playing against himself.
He has yet to recognize that falling
away, that falling from
him so complete it has no counter movement,
that vanishing which is life's first law,
that movement without return,
that leaving powered by a power preceding
all human muster. Without
that recognition, he'll never learn what counts.
But he's still at the beginning.
He'll have to be forgiven.

For now, his joy climbs higher
the deeper toward longing he crouches
before lunging.

HIS LIKENESS

I'm more or less real.
What about you?

As material as time,
and as fugitive
as happiness.

As lasting as sadness, I'm as sound
as memory
and forgetting.
Immutable as water, air, earth, and fire,

I more or less exist.
What do you
tell yourself about being
and being gone?

Co-substantial with lightning,
longing, dreaming, and thinking,
the very stuff of desire,
loneliness, and love, I'm a thought

God entertains about music and death,
color and number,
figure and ground,
legend and consequence.

I'm a proof God is distilling
(I don't know who

or what works you), bringing to bear
all of God's time,

God's happiness,
God's sadness,
God's desire,
God's loneliness,

God's love. Exhausted,
God slips me unfinished
under God's pillow.

I steep as long as God sleeps.
And Time is a black butterfly, pinned

while someone searches for its name in a book.

HIDDEN HEARING

God slips His likeness of me under His pillow.
Morning grows cloudy, the house darkens,
and I know what the rain at the sill is saying:

Be finished with resemblances. Your lamp
hides the light. A voice,
being a voice and not the wind,
can't carry anything away. And yet,
it makes any land a place, a country
of the air, and laughter its seventh day.

Last night I dreamed of voices in a grove.
Ladders reaching from the ground into the branches.
I was mending my children's coats,
worrying if the light would last
long enough for me to thread the needle.

It's spacious beneath God's pillow,
where I nod with the trees in the wind,
listen to the rain,
and count the seconds
between the lightning and the thunder,

deaf to former things,
unencumbered of things to come,
leaving God to recoup
a human fate.

God snores, His slumber immense
and musty with the season's litter.

God rolls over in His sleep
and churns the seabed
to dislodge many buried keys.

Outside, a bird is telling time's green name.
It stops when I stop to listen,
and starts again as soon as I give up
holding my breath to hear it,
as though wholehearted listening intrudes
where hearing ajar makes room for singing
so tender my attention snuffs it,
or else so brimming
my ear's least turning spills it.

Sooner or later, God will again
bear out that semblance He makes of me each day.
He'll knead, fold, punch, pull, mark, smudge,
erase, and tear away.

Sometimes it feels like love.
And makes me tremble.
Sometimes it hurts like death.
And makes me shake.

AT THE YEAR'S REVOLVING DOOR

It's just time,
the book I read, the letter I write,
the window I look out of.

It's just a needle I thread,
a sleeve I keep trying to mend,
the spool diminishing.

It's just my one hand writing words,
my other hand weighing
the silences between them.

It's just time inside of time, the future inside
the seeds inside the pulp
of the apple I eat, skin and all, seeds and everything.

And the fruit rotting on the ground?
Time unraveling.
And time folded smaller and smaller.

And the fruit expected
overhead? Time
appointed and appointing.

And when it is time,
I will hear the name fire and air
assign to each bowed head of grass.

And when it is time, I will remind myself:
All of the light is one, unanimous with the dark.
Every world is two: inside and outside.
Time is many:

the voices of children in the playground
shouting out the stations of their games,
the specific gravity of my hands
setting the table at evening,
the names of the guests
on my mind, the names of the missing become
so many questions
arising at the year's revolving door.

Time is almost our home.
The seasons almost tell a story.
The seasons groan in the bedded hinges of our bones.
An original motive in our blood, their wheels turn,
a branching lathe and music
the living, the dead, and the unborn
step in and out of, shadowing each other;
a spiral economy bound to the coursing stars,
whose glacial rungs the dew climbs down
to dwell beside our sleep.

In the meantime, the wind in the garden changes
from agent of a far end to vagrant
turning over the leaves, looking for a story.

Once upon a time,
we were lonely children in a river valley,
and teachers and schoolmates getting our names wrong
helped to keep us hidden, safe
to make the most faithful companions of God and death.
No wonder we were ruined
for any other company.

Now, as then, the one invents our games,
while the other spurs our delicious cries
by keeping every prize in jeopardy.

Then, and now, the wind
in the trees makes the sound
of the turning pages of our nights and days,
the shadows of birds intermittent,
causing restlessness in the living.

LEAVING

Each day, less leaves
in the tree outside my window.
More leave, and every day
more sky. More of the far,
and every night more stars.

Day after shortening day, more
day in my panes, more missing
in the branches, fewer places
for the birds to hide, their abandoned nests exposed.
And night after increasing night,
the disappearances multiply.

The leaves leap from fire
to colder fire,
from belonging to darker belonging,
from membership to ownership.

Their growing absence
leaves no lack, nothing wanting,
and their gone outnumbers their going
through the door they leave ajar.

EAVESDROPPING AT MORNING'S SILL

Risen, says the sun.

The world is your true body,
say the stars, seen and unseen.
But you won't find your mind there.

Little Clock, stop counting, says the sky.

Little Candle, don't look back, says the waning moon.

And the wind charges, *Herd the flowers!*
Pawn style, stigma, stamen, gnomon, and nodus
for compass, sails, and rigging, and more of the map!

And the river reminds,
Those nights were not wasted
when you, a child, undefended
inside and out, lay sleepless under roof beams
older than yourself
and listened to boughs more old,
arched over the house, cracking and groaning
in a wind without age.

Suddenly, the riverbank erupts in bird-calls
to crowd morning's stanza. Dandelion seeds fill the air
and cross the moving water on a high breeze,
each glinting with its share of the dawn,
each waving to the man who watches them leave
one bank for the other, leaving him
to wonder:

How does a man know when
it's safe to sing
and when it's good to cross wide water?
At what threshold do inklings nurse
before they rear
and bridge as voices to decide
what we call level,
pitch, round, square, path, home, and meeting?

THE WORD FROM HIS SONG

The sparrow on my rooftop shouts,
All roads be blessed!

His voice is a ring
for the finger of the beloved.

And he wouldn't work harder at his song
if all the world prized it,

nor temper what sounds like ardor
if a public thought him wrong.

He says singing redeems the body's loneliness.
Flying fixes the heart to the sky's wheel.

Salt cures the spirit.
Light is a fractal script.

Imagination is branched, flowering,
and each fans the buds himself.

He says every atom is burning.
Hunger mends the kingdom by rending,

marrying voices and wings.
Singing builds a throne for hearing,

sets up a swing
between our one night and our day.

It's all song, he says, all singing,
the body's seat and number, the mind's pleats, time's hem.

The voice is a sighted brink.
Its mission is to sort the world.

The tongue is a mortal flower.
The dew at last. The guests arrive.

The child learns his name,
a virgin bell.

And even that iron note
is God awake in two worlds.

God seeks a destiny in all things fired
in the kiln of the sun or the mind.

That's the word from his song.

ALL ABOUT THE BIRDS

Not one of them ever said your name.
Stop putting words in the mouths of the birds.
It's seeds they want.

What are they going to do with words,
tearful drops of theophanic honey,
metaphysical spit, sacrificial blood, endogenous
balsam, camphor, and myrrh, words?

Such an evanescent diet would only leave them
wondering why they're born
and why they die.

A regimen that sweet, salty, and bitter,
that liminal, and next thing you know
they'll be raising airy shrines
and vaulted altars near the sun. Next thing
you know, they'll forget all about sleep
and begin writing histories of their tribes,
chronicling the conquests and the defeats,
the building of their first cities,
the years they were strangers in their own country,
the years they were strangers in a strange land,
the winged expulsions, and the flying returns.
Next thing, they'll be preaching
the chief end of wings and the reign of love.

All because you put words in their mouths.
Stop putting ideas in their heads.
It's you who wants to know the origin of numbers, not them.
It's you who can't find your way home, not them.

It's you who forgets more and more of your first language
each day, you who let the unspoken grow
between you and your mother each year.
It's you who lost the first songs she taught you.
Not the birds.

They might spend most of their days in the sky,
but every evening they remember
to come back to earth.
Not a single one of them ever got lost up high.
It's you who followed your dead there.
And when they remained above, it was you
made it back only three quarters of the way.

And now you can't make sense of living in time,
or of being in a lightless body of murmurs and humming,
earth packed with fire and shot through with longing.
It's you. It's not the birds.
It was never about the birds.

IV

what the moths must eat,
the ants carry away,
the Caesars keep.

She's a breathing remnant
restored to springtime's living cloth.

She's a pair of scissors
trimming lament
to allow for all I don't know.

And I can tell by the markings on her coat
and her black eyes
she knows which dreams to parse,
which to heed, and which to bury.

And look at those prehistoric feet.
No doubt, she's realized the secret to surviving
her own tribe's slaughter and dispersal.

Pocket dictionary
packed with signs in another language,
blazing shard of the original emanation,
pre-Cambrian spark deposit,
igneous jot of infinite magnitude,
fiery iota,

something about her precise little beak
convinces me she grasps degree,
and knows which *i*'s to dot
and which to leave large and alone.

There are words, I say,
and there is The Word.

Every word is a fluctuating flame
to a wick that dies.

But The Word, The Word
is a ruling sum and drastic mean,
the standard that travels
without moving.

Words move,
but The Word is fixed,
the true blank.

The Word is the voice of the lamp,
and words are soot blackening the glass.

The movements of words engender time and death.
But The Word lives outside of time and death.
Inside time, death rules.
Life is death's kingdom.
We live at dying's rate.
Words are a sop for death.
But The Word is the mother of thresholds,
regulating life and death.

The Word begets presences impossible
to confirm,
given the blinding action of time
and the sea and the earth's
turning repose.

And who is that supposed to feed?
Whose thirst would that quench?

She screeches, her voice materializing
a greater body of innumerable birds arriving at dominion,
increasing to overwhelm every mile of my heart,

that bloody aerie branching and leafing,
her feathers become all eyes and mouths,
her voice coming now from everywhere,
booming,

When the Lover is ready,
the Beloved will appear!

Say what's The Word or we both die!

2.

I'll call her my battle angel, this evangelion.
Seraphic herald of the ninth echelon,
pleromatic eon demanding a founding gnosis,
her voice electric tekhelet, Septuagint, a two-leaved door
opening onto porches, chambers, and courts,
her voice a Solomonic column of barley sugar.

She's why I'm crazy.
She's why I can't sleep. She's why I never
sleep. She's why I avoid people.
She's why I drill the eight limbs with the mud-step,
why I walk the octagon of trigrams inscribed on Wudang,
why I practice the Spiral Ox Jaw and the Tiger's Mouth.
She's why I'm hard to live with
and why I say,

The bread that rises in a house that fails,
The Word, father of zero and one,
is our advocate.

A shut eye we name Beginning,
The Word sleeps,
and all is darkness.

An open eye
we name The Treasure,
The Word wakes
and voices are heard among the sounds of water.

The Word dreams, and worlds appear.
And stars beyond and behind our eyes.
And the moon with its hair tied up
and its hair let down.

Bound on every side,
and wide open in the center,
The Word hosts our breath, our span, the space
of our dreaming and our thinking,
our stillness and our moving. And the emerging present
is one of its bodies.

The fulcrum, the eye, the heart enthroned,
the dove without person, homing, The Word

is a hammer raining down its songs,
a river pouring out of the mouth of the anvil.

Twin and unlike, The Word is without peer.
Black and white, it is a wheeling pair
of coincident opposites turning on a point:
Existence and Non-existence hand in hand.
Substance and Void begetting life and death.

The Word is an open book,
and its first and last pages are missing.

It is a brother and sister
telling each other
the missing parts
of one another's stories.

It is the lover and the beloved
constantly changing places in the fire.

And it is the wind in the treetops
outside our window,
a voice torn to pieces. Hear it?

The wind without a house, she says.
Time without a gate, she says.

A memory of the ocean
torments the trees,
a homesickness, she says.

The wind is leafing through both of our histories,
looking for a happy ending.

It is my hand moving over your body, I say,
finding more and more to know.

It is a circle of women
reciting in the round
the oldest stories of Death disguised as a traveler
or overlooked familiar, friend we shunned
for less faithful playmates.

It is a house,
and from inside come the voices of children
taking turns reading to one another.
It is their own story they read.

But why do their voices seem uneasy?
Does the moon, giant
at the window, frighten them?

Does death run amok through all
the pages of the story?
Do the pages turn by themselves?
Are there strangers in the house?
Is the house burning?

Soldiers with guns are at our door again.
Sister, quick. Change into a penny.
I'll fold you in a handkerchief,
put you in my pocket,
and jump inside a sack of rice,
one of the uncooked kernels.

Men with knives are looking in our windows again.
Brother, hurry. Turn yourself
into one of our mother's dolls
sitting on the living room shelf. I'll be the dust
settling on your eyelids.

The ones wearing wings are in the yard.

The ones adorned with lightning are in the house.

The ones decorated with stars
are dividing our futures among them.

Don't answer when they call to us in the voice of Nanny.

Don't believe them when they promise sugar.

Don't come out until evening,
or when you hear our mother weeping to herself.

If only I could become the mirror in her purse,
I'd never come back until the end of time.

3.

The treetops buck and heave
in the night wind.
Like drunks at sea leaning
too far over a rocking bulwark.
Like a woman throwing her green and gold hair
in time to a song only she can hear.

And from inside
that windswept bulk growing darker
comes a frenzied uproar
of what must be
hundreds of hidden birds.

All that noise
of wind, leaves, and branches,
all that uttering from unseen throats,
and is there no word?

All that shrieking, iterating, crying
in the rustling leaves. All that screaming,
shrilling, running din
of squeaky wheels, radiant numbers of tongues,
beaks, hubs, wings, spokes
keening in centrifugal spinning,
and not one word?
Not any? Nor part? No bearing?

One hunger, a fanned fire, roars
in the voice of the sea.

One light eats itself, unconsumed.

The wind is taking the night apart, she says.
The wind is dismantling
the leaves, the branches, the minutes, our listening,

and finding more and more
moving pieces to index:
our hands, our mouths, our voices, recurring stairs

of an imperfect past,
a rumored present,
figures multiplying inside a mirror.

Each, alone
in his dream of the world, I say,
is host and guest, a book
and the one who reads it
by the light of a vanished childhood.

Don't say that, she says.
We see by the light of who we are.
Look at us: You inside me
inside you. We've lived inside
each other from the beginning.
And from before beginning.
Before the world was ever found.

Before the world was found, I say,
I dwelled inside you,
and you breathed all through me,
in my body and its happiness,
in my body and its loneliness.

After I found the world, I had to go
looking for you. Ever since the world,
I only lose you and find you.
Lose you. And find you.

The body of the beloved
is the lover's true homeland, she says.

I can hear you, but I can't hear me, I say,
your voice a burning gown of song and time,
and me with my ghosts, me with my mockingbird.

Don't say that, she says.

What is my mind, I wonder,
but the reflected light of your

voice, O burning one, O seeing voice, O
speaking eye that renders us

now legible,
now indecipherable, now
strangers traveling
under assumed names.

Don't say that, she says.
Look. A single page of the wind
copied by hand
is the volume of despair
the smallest living wing displaces.
And your voice will be your cup
each day my wings shelter
your dear, momentary earth.

My mind is several minds, I say,
each abiding differently: in your eyes,
in the smell of your hair, in your voice
moving over me, in my voice moving over you.

She says, Don't look at your hands.
Watch the shadows they make.
I say, Moving over you, my voice crosses
out of forbidden chambers of the Emperor of China,

through chronicles of exile and death in a foreign country,
to touch the ground I touch in me
when I speak to you.

She says, A new mind makes the world new.
True words are a little blue.
And being human makes the saddest music in the world.

She says, Postpone all morning bells.
The ore lies awake inside the rock, a dream
of origin waiting to be rescued.

I say, The glare of your nakedness
confounds me, a distraction
from the darker incandescence of your being.
Inside you is the safest place to be.

The radio in the kitchen is stuck
in the year I was born.
The capitals of the world are burning.

And of all the things on my mind this evening,
words weigh the least,
Death weighs the most,
and your voice's body
beneath my voice's moving hand
is a green agent of freedom and order,
best friend to my earth and my ache.

Of all the things keeping me from sleep,
words weigh too much, yet not enough.
Time weighs nothing at all,
but I can't bear it.
And your body, burdened by minutes
and ancient rites, is my favorite sad song.

One wave that gives rise to three, shoulder, hip, and knee,
your body is the Lord's pure geometry.
Disguised as Time, your body is tears, lilies,
and the mouth of the falls.

And of all the things we're dying from tonight,
being alive is the strangest.
Surviving our histories is the saddest.
Time leaves the smallest wounds,
and your body, a mortal occasion
of timeless law,
is all the word I know.

SANDALWOOD

The ash keeps dropping from the incense stick.

I keep turning you over in my mind.
I keep turning you over in my heart.

The stick shortens, burning.
The ash grows
and falls.

I keep turning you over.
I keep turning you.
I keep turning.

The ash keeps falling, piling up, more
of the silent reduction.
Burning earns such clean wages,
eye of ember, eye of ash hastening.

I keep turning your eyes over
to find your thoughts.
Turning your voice over
to find your meaning.
Turning your body over to find
a place to hide me.

And you keep turning inside me.

ACKNOWLEDGMENTS

Grateful acknowledgment is made to the editors of the publications where some of the poems in this book previously appeared.

American Poetry Review: "The Undressing"

Harvard Divinity Bulletin: "Hidden Hearing"

Image Journal: "Folding a Five-Cornered Star So the Corners Meet," "I Loved You Before I Was Born," "At the Year's Revolving Door"

Poetry: "Changing Places in the Fire," "Three Words"

World Literature Today: "God Is Burning"

The Best American Poetry 2016: "Folding a Five-Cornered Star So the Corners Meet"

A small handful of the poems in this book previously appeared together as a chapbook titled *The Word from His Song*, published by BOA Editions, Ltd. in 2016.

I am grateful to *Poetry* magazine for recognizing "Changing Places in the Fire" with the Levinson Award.

I would also like to express my sincere gratitude to Hollins University for a residency that greatly contributed to my completing this book.

To my wife and family, thank you for your nurturance, your unflagging love and support.

To Jill Bialosky, thank you for your belief in my work, and for not giving up on me.

I LOVED YOU BEFORE I WAS BORN

I loved you before I was born.
It doesn't make sense, I know.

I saw your eyes before I had eyes to see.
And I've lived longing
for your every look ever since.
That longing entered time as this body.
And the longing grew as this body waxed.
And the longing grows as this body wanes.
That longing will outlive this body.

I loved you before I was born.
It makes no sense, I know.

Long before eternity, I caught a glimpse
of your neck and shoulders, your ankles and toes.
And I've been lonely for you from that instant.
That loneliness appeared on earth as this body.
And my share of time has been nothing
but your name outrunning my ever saying it clearly.
Your face fleeing my ever
kissing it firmly once on the mouth.

In longing, I am most myself, rapt,
my lamp mortal, my light
hidden and singing.

I give you my blank heart.
Please write on it
what you wish.

ADORE

(adore, verb, from Latin, *adorare*,
from *ad-* 'to' + *orare-* 'speak, call, pray')

You lie asleep beside me,
one hand on the pillow and cupped
at your mouth, as if to tell a secret.

As if you might say in your sleep
what you could never find
words for awake.

Or as if you called
across a din of other voices,
or the howl of empty space. Calling

because there are no bells
to strike the hours where we live. And I must know
when to kneel and when to rise.
What to praise and what to curse.
I must know how to bless
and how to receive blessing.

One hand on your pillow and cupped
at your mouth,
as if you spoke a word
you'd kept to yourself all day, waiting
for your most unguarded moment
to say, a thought meant for me, meant to be
shared between us this way,
sealed this way, a secret

no voice can carry without destroying,
a word without carriage, except conveyed
in the peace of your body and face,

a word born out of your deepest rest, a word
which only my own deepest breathing
and happiest rest beside you,
face to face, free of thinking, can sustain.

Maybe you had to be asleep
to say what you knew to be true.
Or what you had to say
you might not could bear to hear,
and so must say so softly
I must close my eyes, I must turn
inward, to where you've made a room
and a bed inside me, to receive it.

You say:
We cannot look upon Love's face without dying.
So we face each other to see Love's look.
And thus third-person souls
suddenly stand at gaze
and the lover and the beloved,
second- and first-persons,
You and I, eye
to eye, are born.
But such refraction, multiplying gazes, strews
Love's eye upon the objects of the world,
as upon the objects of our room.

My brush, hairpin, mirror, book,
your loving look finds each of these things
lovable, I can see. Things
by any other measure poor, your look crowns
to make them your heart's royalty.

Face, blush, breath, eyes, evanescent,
pledged to death, nowhere stored,
Love's look gathers within its fondling
to adore.

This strewing and gathering
of Love's face, of Love's gaze, and only this,
begun in death's audience, is the founding
action, call it the fundamental
paradise . . . did I say paradise?
I meant paradox . . . the fundamental paradox
of the breaths we breathe,
the thoughts we witness,
the kisses we exchange,
and every poem you write.